W9-BXA-605

THE SOUTHERN HOME FRONT
OF THE CIVIL WAR

ROBERTA BAXTER

Heinemann Library
Chicago, Illinois

www.heinemannraintree.com
Visit our website to find out more information about Heinemann-Raintree books.

To order:
☎ Phone 888-454-2279
💻 Visit www.heinemannraintree.com
to browse our catalog and order online.

©2011 Heinemann Library
an imprint of Capstone Global Library, LLC
Chicago, Illinois

Edited by Megan Cotugno
Designed by Ryan Frieson
Illustrated by Mapping Specialists, Ltd.
Picture research by Tracy Cummins
Originated by [select]
Printed in [select]

14 13 12 11 10
10 9 8 7 6 5 4 3 2 1

Library of Congress Cataloging-in-Publication Data

Baxter, Roberta, 1952-
 The southern home front of the Civil War / Roberta Baxter.
   p. cm. — (Why we fought: the Civil War)
 Includes bibliographical references and index.
 ISBN 978-1-4329-3912-0 (hc)
 1. Confederate States of America—Social conditions—Juvenile literature. 2. Confederate States of America—History—Juvenile literature. 3. United States—History—Civil War, 1861-1865—Social aspects—Juvenile literature. I. Title.
 F214.B39 2011
 973.7'1—dc22

                    2009050065

Acknowledgments

The author and publishers are grateful to the following for permission to reproduce copyright material:

Corbis pp. 10, 21, 35 (© Corbis), pp. 15, 39 (© Bettmann), 19; Getty Images p. 5; Library of Congress Prints and Photographs Division pp. 7, 8, 12, 17, 24, 27, 29, 30, 31, 33, 37, 40, 41, 42, 43; National Archive pp. 4, 22, 23, 16 (Charters of Freedom); The Art Archive pp. 25 (Culver Pictures), 34 (Massachusetts Commandery Military Order of the Loyal Legion and the US Army Military History Institute); The Bridgeman Art Library International p. 14 (Peter Newark American Pictures); The Granger Collection, New York pp. 11, 13.

Cover photo of Capitol building in Columbia, South Carolina, after destruction in the city during the Civil War reproduced with permission from The Art Archive (Culver Pictures).

We would like to thank Dr. James I. Robertson, Jr. for his invaluable help in the preparation of this book.

Every effort has been made to contact copyright holders of any material reproduced in this book. Any omissions will be rectified in subsequent printings if notice is given to the publisher.

All the Internet addresses (URLs) given in this book were valid at the time of going to press. However, due to the dynamic nature of the Internet, some addresses may have changed, or sites may have changed or ceased to exist since publication. While the author and Publishers regret any inconvenience this may cause readers, no responsibility for any such changes can be accepted by either the author or the Publishers.

Contents

Throughout this book, you will find green text boxes that contain facts and questions to help you interact with a primary source. Use these questions as a way to think more about where our historical information comes from.

Some words are shown in bold, **like this**. You can find out what they mean by looking in the glossary, on page 46.

Why Did We Fight the Civil War?

The thirteen colonies had united to fight the **Revolutionary War**. However, parts of the United States remained very different in culture, **economy**, and views. The North wanted a strong central government. People in Southern states stressed the idea of **states' rights**. This meant that states had the power to determine their own laws without the **federal** government telling them what to do. The South felt that since the states united to form the **Union**, they could also make the decision to split from the Union, or **secede**.

A soldier in the Union army lifts a battered flag. The Civil War was a long and bloody conflict between the North and the South.

Slavery in the South

Slavery was a huge part of the disagreement between North and South. **Plantation** owners in the South could only grow and harvest their crops of cotton, tobacco, and rice with the help of slaves. They had always owned slaves and saw no reason to change the system. Factories in the North treated employees little better than slaves, but they did pay wages. **Immigrants** flowing into the northern United States took low-paying jobs and worked their way up to the middle class. Industries expanded, bringing in more money and more jobs.

Meanwhile, the South continued on as before, with little growth. The people of the South knew that the North was quickly passing them in population and wealth. The North would be in control of the federal government, and the South could do nothing to stop this.

Southern plantations required many slaves to work the fields, care for the house, and tend children.

5

As people pushed westward, new territories were formed. Arguments sprang up about whether **slavery** would be permitted in these areas. Before the Civil War, Congress reached several **compromises** that helped preserve the **Union**, for a time.

CHART OF COMPROMISES

- Missouri Compromise of 1820: Missouri was admitted to the Union as a slave state, but a line was drawn so that slavery would not be permitted in any new states formed from land north of Missouri's southern border.

- Compromise of 1850: California was admitted as a free state; the territories of New Mexico and Utah could decide about slavery; and the Fugitive Slave Act was strengthened, making it against the law to help an escaped slave.

- Kansas-Nebraska Act: Kansas and Nebraska were to decide for themselves about whether to allow slavery.

This map shows the division of North and South during the Civil War.

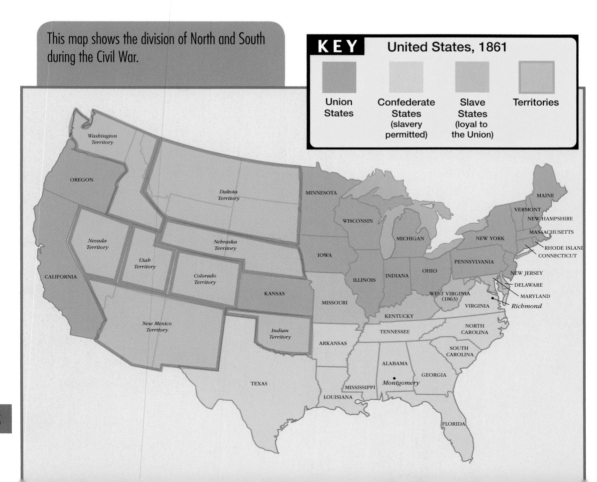

KEY — United States, 1861

Union States | Confederate States (slavery permitted) | Slave States (loyal to the Union) | Territories

These acts of Congress did not satisfy either the North or the South, but each side gained a little of what they wanted. The Union stayed together, though the arguments continued.

Presidential Election

When the presidential election of 1860 approached, the Democratic Party was split among several candidates. A new party, the Republicans, nominated Abraham Lincoln of Illinois. He said that the **Constitution** could not destroy slavery where it already existed, but he pledged to stop its spread. "On that point," he said, "hold firm, as with a chain of steel."

Lincoln won the election. People in the South saw his election as a tragedy for their part of the country. In Southern cities, straw men made to look like Lincoln were burned on courthouse lawns.

Lawmakers in the South began debating the idea of pulling out of the United States to form their own country. South Carolina voted to secede on December 20, 1860. Other Southern states soon followed.

Southerners did not believe Lincoln when he said he would not try to abolish slavery in their states.

Who Led the South During the War?

On February 9, 1861, Jefferson Davis was elected president of the **Confederate States of America**. He and his wife, Varina, were in their garden on their **plantation** in Mississippi when the telegram announcing his presidency arrived. Davis knew that he faced a long struggle ahead of him and that governing the Confederacy would be difficult.

Jefferson Davis was born on June 3, 1808, in Kentucky. His family moved to a cotton plantation in Mississippi when he was still a baby. Davis's family sent him to the best schools. When he was 16, Davis attended the United States Military Academy at West Point, New York. He graduated as an army lieutenant in 1828.

**Primary Source:
Jefferson Davis, 1861**

Jefferson Davis was elected president of the Confederate States of America in 1861.

Thinking About the Source:

What do you notice first about this image?

Davis is surrounded by a wreath of corn, tobacco, and flowers.

Why do you think the newspaper chose to frame the portrait of Davis in this way?

Davis served in the western territories for seven years and then returned to the family plantation. However, when war broke out with Mexico in 1846, he rejoined the army. After Davis returned from Mexico, he served as a U.S. senator until 1851. He then ran for governor of Mississippi, but was defeated.

Secretary of War

President Franklin Pierce appointed Davis as secretary of war. After Pierce's presidency, Davis again ran for the **U.S. Senate** and served as a senator for Mississippi until 1861. His terms as senator included the times of vigorous debate over **slavery**, **states' rights**, and the **compromises** reached before the Civil War. Davis believed that each state had an unquestionable right to **secede** from the **Union**. However, he argued against secession. Davis believed it would harm the South more than the North.

When Mississippi seceded from the Union, Davis resigned as senator. Soon after, he was elected president of the Confederacy. The years of the Civil War were difficult for Davis. His own **cabinet** and congress argued frequently, and Davis was criticized for the setbacks suffered by Confederate troops. He was often in ill health during the war.

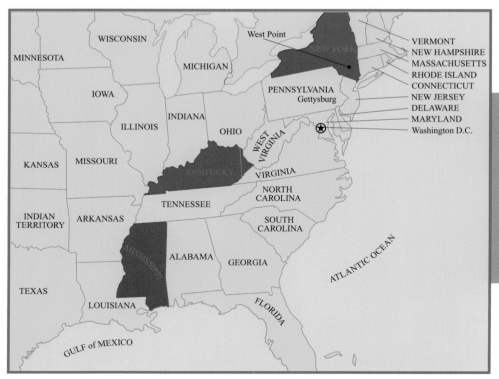

Davis had lived in the Southern state of Mississippi, the border state of Kentucky, and the Northern state of New York. He understood the issues of slavery and states' rights from a variety of viewpoints.

TIMELINE OF JEFFERSON DAVIS

June 3, 1808	Jefferson Davis is born
1828	Graduates from **West Point**
1828	Serves as U.S. army officer assigned to the frontier
1846	Rejoins U.S. army to fight in **Mexican-American War**
1847–1851	Serves as U.S. senator for Mississippi
1853–1857	Serves as U.S. secretary of war
1857–1861	Again serves as senator for Mississippi
January 9, 1861	Mississippi **secedes** from the **Union**
January 1861	Resigns from the **U.S. Senate**
February 9, 1861	Appointed president of the Confederacy
1865	Captured and sent to prison
1867	Released from prison, returns to Mississippi
December 6, 1889	Jefferson Davis dies

Jefferson Davis and three generations of his family sit in the hallway of his home in 1885.

The War Begins

Fort Sumter, a Union fort, was located on an island in the harbor of Charleston, South Carolina. Confederates from nearby Charleston could see the Union flag flying from the fort. Confederate President Jefferson Davis ordered General P. G. T. Beauregard to take the fort. On April 12, 1861, Confederate troops fired cannons at Fort Sumter.

WITNESSING THE BATTLE

Charleston residents witnessed the battle from their rooftops. On April 12, 1861, Mary Boykin Chestnut wrote in her diary "…The shells were bursting…" Later in the day, she added, "we hear nothing, can listen to nothing; boom, boom goes the cannon all the time."

After a day and a half, the Union commander **surrendered**, and the troops were allowed to leave the fort and return to the North. The Union flag was taken down and the rebel flag was flown. Charleston and other Southern towns celebrated. Only one had been killed and two wounded, but the war had begun.

Primary Source: Mary Chestnut

Mary Chestnut lived in Charleston, where she could see and hear the beginning of the Civil War.

Thinking About the Source:

What small details do you notice in this image?

When do you think this photograph was taken?

What Was It Like to Live on a Plantation?

Plantation owners were only a tiny fraction of the Southern population, but they held the majority of the wealth. A major plantation would have as many as 1,000 acres and 50 to 100 slaves. A smaller one would have fewer slaves.

Each plantation was run like a small town. A large house would serve for the plantation family, and slave cabins were constructed for the slaves and their families. Other buildings included barns, storehouses, grain mills, chicken coops, and workshops.

Plantation Work

The main Southern crop was cotton, but rice and tobacco were also grown. Men of the plantation supervised the overseers of the slaves. They bought equipment and livestock, sold their crops, and bought and sold slaves. Slaves were considered valuable property.

Plantation homes were large, reflecting the wealth of the owners.

Women of the plantation supervised the care of the home. Their entertainment consisted of attending balls and sewing circles, and visiting other plantations. After traveling long distances, people often stayed for several weeks. Extra bedrooms were kept ready in plantation homes for any visitors.

Female slaves helped care for the children of the family. Children spent their time playing and studying. Boys learned to shoot at an early age and often hunted and fished. Girls were taught to sew, embroider, and draw. Many families had tutors for their children, and the tutor usually lived in the plantation house.

Leaving to Fight

When the Civil War began, thousands of plantation owners and their sons left to join the Confederate army. Women were left behind to manage the plantations and the slaves. Tutors also enlisted in the Confederate army, so education stopped for most plantation children.

Female slaves of the household were trusted to take care of the children.

13

What Was It Like to Be a Slave?

Slavery had existed in the United States long before the **Revolutionary War**, both in the North and the South. After the **cotton gin** was invented, **plantation** owners began growing cotton. Slaves were needed to plant, weed, and harvest the cotton. Mills in the North and in England were demanding more cotton to make cloth.

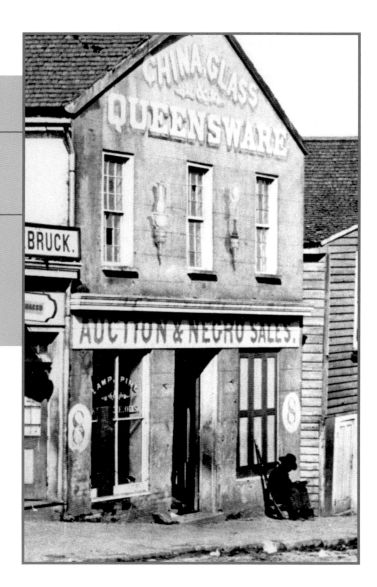

Primary Source: Slave Market

This is a photo of a Southern slave market in Atlanta, Georgia.

Thinking About the Source:

Describe what you see in this image.

What, if any, words can you read?

What other details can you see?

Slavery in the Constitution

When the **Constitutional Convention** met to form a new government in 1787, it discussed slavery. Should slaves be counted in the population of the South? That would put the South far ahead of the North, meaning it would have more representatives in Congress. The **compromise** was made that slaves would count as 3/5 of a person. At the convention it was also decided that bringing slaves from Africa had to stop by 1808, 20 years after **ratification** of the **Constitution**. In 1808 President Thomas Jefferson signed a bill that fulfilled that Constitutional requirement and stopped slaves from being brought to the United States. He and some other Southerners thought slavery would die out.

Even when new slaves were no longer brought into the country, slavery expanded due to the birth of children of slaves. By 1860, there were almost 4 million slaves, mostly in the Southern states. Slaves had no rights. They were bought and sold like property. They could not move to a new job or home. Families could be separated and sold to different owners. It was illegal to teach a slave to read.

Slaves worked in the fields, tending the cotton or tobacco of the owner. The men also cared for animals, repaired equipment, and worked as blacksmiths, gardeners, or in mills. Women cleaned house, cooked, cared for their master's children, and made clothes. Children of slaves were also slaves. At a young age, they were taught to do chores. They gathered eggs, carried wood and water, and fed animals.

Fields of cotton in the South were full of slave workers.

Slaves who tried to escape and got caught were punished severely. The **Underground Railroad** was a network of people dedicated to helping slaves escape to the North. Slaves did not march off to war, but they were often sent to dig trenches, cut wood, and carry water for the Confederate army. Some slaves who escaped enlisted in the Union army.

The Emancipation Proclamation

In September 1862, President Lincoln issued the **Emancipation Proclamation**, which promised freedom to slaves in Confederate states as of January 1863. The law said, "all persons held as slaves within any State or designated part of a State…shall be then, thenceforward, and forever free." Most were not freed until the end of the war.

Finally, on January 31, 1865, after the war was over, the Thirteenth **Amendment** to the Constitution became law. This amendment officially freed all slaves and ended slavery.

The Thirteenth Amendment ended slavery in the United States.

HARRIET TUBMAN (c. 1820–1913)

Harriet Tubman was born as a slave in 1820. She suffered beatings from owners. A weight thrown by an overseer at another slave hit her. The injury caused her health problems for the rest of her life. In 1849, Tubman managed to escape slavery.

Over the next years, she made many trips and guided other slaves to freedom. Her nickname was "Moses," because she led her people to freedom much like Moses in the Bible. She boasted that she never lost a passenger on the Underground Railroad.

Harriet Tubman risked her life to help slaves escape to freedom in the North.

What Was It Like to Live on a Small Farm?

Most of the people of the South lived on small farms, rather than **plantations**. Everyone in the family worked to make the farm produce what they needed. A small farm owner might have no slaves or only one or two.

Farm Work

Men worked in the fields, plowing, planting and harvesting the crops. Owners of small farms might have a few fields of cotton or tobacco, which they sold to have cash money. Other crops were usually food for themselves and their animals.

Women cleaned house, tended the garden and chickens, and prepared food. Each week there was bread to be baked, butter to churn, and washing to do. Food was preserved each summer for the winter months. Fibers of cotton or wool were spun into thread, woven into cloth, and sewed into clothes for the whole family. Women also made soap at home and candles for light.

OFF TO WAR

Men from small farms also marched off to war, leaving women and children struggling to handle the farm tasks. On January 1, 1862, Virginia citizen Celina Wesley Combs wrote to her Confederate soldier husband, "I have got the corn all secured [harvested and stored]. I did not get any rye sowed."

Boys usually fed and watered animals, cleaned the barns, brought in firewood and water, and gathered eggs. They also hunted and fished to add to the food supply, and worked in the fields with their fathers. Girls might also gather eggs, milk cows, pick vegetables, and feed the chickens.

Children might attend school in a nearby schoolhouse or be taught by their parents. In the evenings, families gathered around a fire. Someone might read aloud while the mothers and older sisters sewed or knitted, and the fathers and older brothers mended a harness or shelled nuts.

The South had more small farms than large plantations.

What Were Southern Cities Like During the War?

The cities of the South were smaller than those in the North. New Orleans, Louisiana, was the largest city, followed by Charleston, South Carolina, and Richmond, Virginia. Only one (New Orleans) of the top ten largest cities in the nation was in the South. About 10 percent of the people of the South lived in cities.

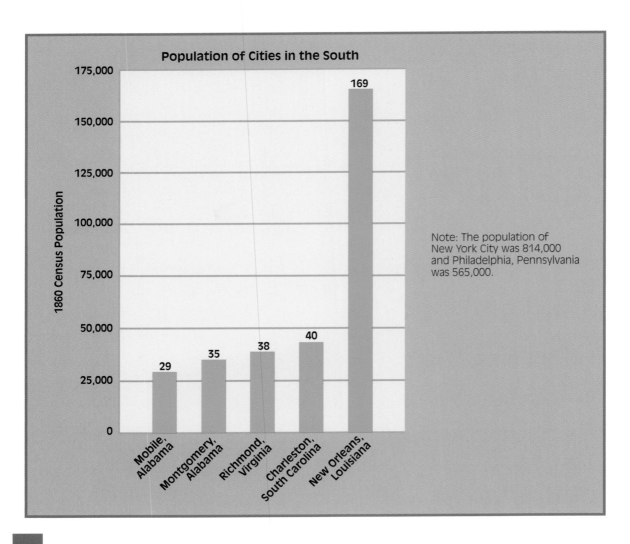

Note: The population of New York City was 814,000 and Philadelphia, Pennsylvania was 565,000.

The port city of New Orleans was valuable to the South, until it was captured by the Union during the war.

People in Southern cities worked jobs similar to those in Northern cities. The men were lawyers, doctors, and merchants. Many cities had harbors where ships docked daily, bringing items from around the world and shipping out cotton. City houses varied between three-story mansions and simple huts.

Even though they did not have fields like farm families, people in the city often had vegetable gardens, chickens, cows, horses, and pigs. Children living in cities might not have as many chores as farm children, but they still gathered eggs and fed animals.

Some cities had factories, but the South did not have nearly as many factories as the North. The South could not make as many guns, cannonballs, and uniforms during the war. The lack of industrial strength crippled the South during the Civil War. Destroyed or lost cannons and rifles could not be easily replaced, and the supply of ammunition and cannonballs was often very low. The Tregedar Iron Works of Richmond, Virginia, cast 1,099 cannons during the war, but it was not enough to match **Union** production.

Will These Inventions Work?

War often leads to new technology. The Civil War was a good example of this. Both the North and South used railroads to carry troops and supplies into battle for the first time. Railroads became targets, and many were destroyed. Union General William Tecumseh Sherman's forces destroyed railroads by tearing loose the rails, heating them up, and wrapping them around tree trunks. The results were jokingly called "Sherman's neckties."

Ironclad Ships

The Confederates took a wooden ship and bolted iron plates onto the **hull**, turning it into the **ironclad** CSS *Virginia*. The **Union** government had John Ericsson build a federal ironclad, the USS *Monitor*. In 1862, a battle between the two ironclads happened at Hampton Roads, Virginia. The *Virginia* sunk several Union ships. However, when the two ironclads fired at each other, and even collided, little damage occurred. After four hours, the *Virginia* pulled away. The Confederates later burned and sank the *Virginia* when they had to leave the area.

Railroad tracks were destroyed wherever armies went during the Civil War, to break enemy supply lines.

Submarines

The Confederates also had the first submarines. Torpedo boats known as "*Davids*" floated very low in the water and carried a "torpedo" (what we would call a mine) on a pole at the front. In one attack, the *David* exploded its torpedo against the hull of a Union ship, *New Ironsides*, and caused enough damage for the Union ship to need to be docked for repairs.

Horace L. Hunley built a submarine called the *H.L. Hunley*. A crew of nine propelled the sub underwater by turning a crank with their hands. During sea trials, the *Hunley* sank several times, and many crewmembers, including Hunley, were killed. However, on February 17, 1864, the *Hunley* and her crew snuck across Charleston Harbor with a torpedo on a pole at the front of the sub. The *Hunley* banged into the hull of the USS *Housatonic*, and the explosion sank the Union warship. The *Hunley*, damaged by the explosion, also sank, along with her crew.

Primary Source:
Torpedo Boat

A Southern torpedo gunboat is pictured here in Charleston in 1865.

Thinking About the Source:

Describe what you see.

What do you think happened to this torpedo boat?

What Other Effects Did War Have on the Home Front?

The first major battle of the war, called the Battle of Bull Run by the **Union** and the Battle of Manassas by the Confederacy, was fought on July 21, 1861. Bull Run was a small creek about 40 kilometers (25 miles) south of Washington, DC. As the Union troops marched out of Washington, they were joined by **civilians** and government officials who wanted to see the battle. They thought the Confederates would be quickly beaten and the war over after one battle.

The Confederates Win

After several hours of fighting, fresh Confederate troops reached the battlefield and began pushing the tired Union troops back. The retreat became a panic, and both Union soldiers and civilians fled in a confused mass. It became known as "the great skedaddle." The Confederates defeated the Union troops and controlled the battlefield. The South rejoiced, thinking that the war was over. In Richmond, Virginia, capital of the Confederacy, a 100-gun salute celebrated the victory.

The North named the battle after a creek known as Bull Run. The South named it after the nearby town of Manassas.

The **economy** of the South depended on the sale of cotton to make money. The Union navy **blockaded** the ports of the South, stopping ships from entering or leaving. No cotton could be sold to the mills of England and the North. Bales of cotton piled up on docks, while Confederate **plantation** owners grew even more cotton that could not be sold.

Without the ability to ship and sell it, cotton piled up in the South.

BLOCKADE RUNNERS

Fast ships known as blockade runners managed to slip past the Northern blockade and bring supplies to the South. Ships with names like *Banshee, Mars, Leopard, Jeff Davis,* and *Lady Davis* evaded the Union navy and carried cotton to Bermuda or Nassau. They returned with clothes, manufactured goods, and over 6,000 rifles. Union ships sank or seized about 1,500 blockade runners, but some continued to run the blockade. They could not carry enough supplies to support the South, but their efforts were profitable for ship owners and a great **morale** boost for the Confederacy.

The Union blockaded all of the South's major seaports.

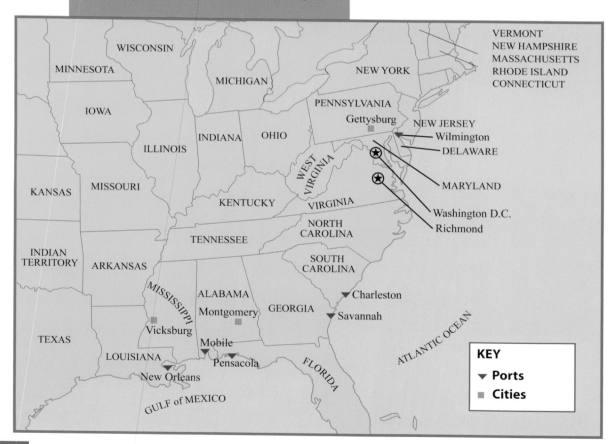

VERMONT
NEW HAMPSHIRE
MASSACHUSETTS
RHODE ISLAND
CONNECTICUT

WISCONSIN
MINNESOTA
MICHIGAN
NEW YORK
IOWA
PENNSYLVANIA
Gettysburg
NEW JERSEY
INDIANA   OHIO
ILLINOIS
Wilmington
DELAWARE
KANSAS   MISSOURI
WEST VIRGINIA
MARYLAND
KENTUCKY
VIRGINIA
Washington D.C.
Richmond
NORTH CAROLINA
TENNESSEE
SOUTH CAROLINA
INDIAN TERRITORY   ARKANSAS
MISSISSIPPI   ALABAMA
Charleston
Montgomery   GEORGIA
Savannah
Vicksburg
TEXAS
Mobile
LOUISIANA   Pensacola
New Orleans
ATLANTIC OCEAN
FLORIDA
GULF of MEXICO

KEY
▼ Ports
■ Cities

Inflation during the war caused Confederate money to be worthless by 1865.

Printing Money

Before the war, the most common money was gold or silver coins. Once the war started in 1861, the Confederacy began printing Confederate bills. Individual states and banks later printed their own paper money and issued it to be used for payment. As the war continued, there were so many bills floating around the Confederacy that they lost their value. At the end of the war, they were worthless.

As the war continued, **inflation** caused rising costs for everything. A pound of bacon cost 12.5 cents in 1861, and $11 to $13 in 1865. Potatoes went from 75 cents a bushel to $25. Flour cost up to $1,000 a barrel. People were unable to buy clothing or shoes and had to make their own with whatever they could find.

The people of the home front in the South did not only suffer from **inflation**. Most of the battles of the Civil War were fought across the South, causing damage to farms and **plantations**, and forcing people to leave. As Union soldiers captured more of the South, plantation homes became headquarters for Union troops. Other plantations were burned or destroyed in fighting, leaving the owners with no place to live.

Bread Riot

On April 2, 1863, hungry, angry women gathered in Richmond, Virginia, to ask the governor for lower prices for food. The group began marching through the city streets. More women joined, until they became a mob. They began breaking windows and chanting, "Bread, bread, bread."

President Jefferson Davis stood in a wagon and threw what money he had out to the crowd. He told them it was all he had, and that they must go home, or he would send the **militia** after them. The mob broke up, but the leaders were arrested, and some were put in prison.

Farms and homes were destroyed by the actions of enemy troops. The destruction of farms brought more fleeing people to the cities to find protection. It also meant that there was less food, because the grains and other crops had been burned in the fields.

Burning the Shenandoah Valley

During the final fighting in the fertile Shenandoah Valley of Virginia in 1864, Union soldiers under the command of General Philip Sheridan destroyed towns, fields, and barns. Sheridan's campaign was so devastating that it is called "The Burning." In his report, General Sheridan said his troops burned 2,000 barns, 120 mills, and about 500,000 bushels of grain. This destruction left the Confederate army low on supplies, and meant that many citizens had no bread or meat.

Primary Source:
Ruins at Hampton, Virginia

Many Southern farms, like this one in Hampton, Virginia, were completely destroyed during the Civil War.

Thinking About the Source:

What do you notice first about this photo?

Who do you think the man in the photo is?

New Orleans fell to the Union army in April 1862. Vicksburg, also on the Mississippi River, was now the last city blocking the North from full control of the river. Abraham Lincoln called it the key of the Confederacy. If the city was captured, the South could no longer transport supplies using the Mississippi River. General Ulysses S. Grant was sent to capture Vicksburg. Located high on a cliff overlooking the Mississippi River, the city was such a strong fortress that Union troops could not capture it. So General Grant's soldiers surrounded the city and cut it off from all supplies.

Ulysses S. Grant was a determined and successful commander for the Union.

Vicksburg was under siege for 47 days. People dug and moved into caves to be away from the Union shells. The city ran out of food and finally **surrendered**. General Grant's troops entered the defeated city on July 4, 1863.

LUCY MCRAE

Lucy McRae's family was trapped in the city during the siege. They also lived in a cave. Lucy remembered a night when a shell landed on top of their cave: "This caused a large mass of earth to slide… catching me under it. As soon as the men could get to me, they pulled me from under the mass of earth." Lucy recalled, "Our provisions [food] were becoming scarce… Mother would not eat mule meat, but we children ate some, and it tasted right good, having been cooked nicely."

Lucy's father returned to the cave one evening and said, "You can all come home for a night's rest. General Pemberton has surrendered, and General Grant will enter the city in the morning." She added, "We went home."

The capture of Vicksburg was an important victory for the North and a turning point in the war. A view of the battlefield of Vicksburg is shown above.

WILLIE LORD

Eleven-year-old Willie Lord's family lived in Vicksburg. Like many families, they lived in caves that **civilians** dug out in order to escape Union shells falling in the city. Willie recalled, "… children played while their mothers sewed by candlelight…" Willie Lord's home suffered extensive damage during the siege. His mother grieved to see "every room in the house injured and scarcely a window left whole."

Atlanta Surrenders

In 1864, Atlanta, Georgia, was surrounded by **Union** troops led by General William Tecumseh Sherman. Just as in Vicksburg, food became scarce. Atlanta and the Confederates defending it held on for more than a month. On September 1, the Confederates evacuated Atlanta and Union forces marched in.

Sherman controlled Atlanta, but he planned to destroy the fighting will of the Confederacy. In November, he began what came to be called "Sherman's March to the Sea." As his Union troops left Atlanta, they set fire to the city, and scavengers plundered empty houses. Sherman's army was out of reach of supplies from the North, so they took what they needed from Atlanta and the countryside before burning it.

Sherman's March to the Sea

As the Union soldiers marched southeast through Georgia, they began Sherman's plan, meant to force the Confederacy to ask for peace. Sherman banned his men from plundering the homes, but he did little to stop the action. When they reached a **plantation**, Sherman's troops would seize any food and valuables they could find. If they could not use the animals, they killed them.

A PRESENT

Sherman finally reached the ocean at Savannah, Georgia. On December 22, 1864, he sent President Lincoln a telegram announcing his capture of the city: "…a Christmas-gift… with 150 heavy guns and plenty of ammunition; also, about 25,000 bales of cotton." Sherman's march had covered 462 kilometers (287 miles) of enemy territory and done $100 million in damage to the South.

Primary Source:
Sherman's March to the Sea

General William Tecumseh Sherman led his troops on a destructive march as they left Atlanta, doing little to control them as they set fire to the city and burned the surrounding countryside.

This illustration was created in 1868, four years after Sherman's march.

Thinking About the Source:

Describe what is happening in the image.

Do you think that the illustrator was present at the scene?

If this image was created today, what would be different?

Tending the Wounded and Sick

As battles continued, many Southern women spent hours tending the wounded in hospitals. Sometimes **plantation** homes were near enough to the battlefield that they were used as hospitals.

Sally Tompkins borrowed a spacious home in Richmond, Virginia, to be used as a hospital. She was so efficient as a hospital administrator that Jefferson Davis appointed her a captain in the Confederate army. She did not want to receive army pay, saying it should be saved for the soldiers. More than a thousand wounded soldiers received care under her guidance, but Tompkins refused to accept pay. Only 73 of her patients died—the best survival rate of any hospital, North or South.

Women who had only basic nursing skills were pressed into service. The hospitals were overflowing, not only from those wounded in battle, but also men who got illnesses such as diarrhea, typhoid fever, pneumonia, scarlet fever, and measles.

Women nurses tended the sick and wounded in battlefield hospitals.

Women on the home front did everything they could to help the war effort.

Supplies for the Soldiers

When women were not tending farms or businesses, they were sewing shirts and knitting socks for the soldiers. Girls, slaves, and even boys learned to knit so they could make socks and hats. They also cut and rolled bandages. Boxes of candy, soap, and food supplies were sent from towns all over the South to the soldiers fighting far away.

The people of both sides were tired of war, yet it dragged on. At the beginning of the Civil War, most Southerners thought the war would be over and the soldiers home by Christmas of 1861. Now it was 1865, and still the war went on.

How Did the Civil War End?

As the war continued into 1865, the Confederacy was dying. The Southern cities of New Orleans, Atlanta, Savannah, Vicksburg, and most of the western Confederacy were in the hands of the **Union**. Supplies were running out, so that most of General Robert E. Lee's army was in tatters and hungry. Many people on the Southern home front were also starving.

Columbia, South Carolina, Burns

General Sherman continued his march north into South Carolina. He intended to punish the state that had been the first to **secede**. In February, his troops entered Columbia, South Carolina. The city caught fire on the windy night of February 17, 1865. Some reports said the fires were set by Union troops, but others claimed that Confederates had set cotton bales ablaze to keep them from falling into Union hands. High winds whipped the flames into an inferno that swept the town. Almost all public buildings were destroyed, along with many homes. The city was filled with helpless women and children who were made homeless in a single night.

Richmond Falls

Finally, Union troops approached Richmond, the capital of the Confederacy. Jefferson Davis and the rest of the government fled south, and people clogged the roads as they tried to escape. After the city was captured, Abraham Lincoln came to see the conquered capital. He toured the ruins of the city, and many slaves came out to shake the hand that had freed them.

General Lee still maneuvered his exhausted Confederate troops to keep fighting. However, Union General Ulysses S. Grant blocked his way. The two armies met near the small village of Appomattox Court House. Lee soon realized he was surrounded. He told his aides on April 8, 1865, "There is nothing left for me to do but to go and see General Grant and I would rather die a thousand deaths."

Primary Source:
Charleston, South Carolina, 1865

The city of Charleston was damaged by the war. In this photo, children rest among the ruins.

Thinking About the Source:

Look closely at the image, particularly the background. What do you see?

The city sustained a lot of damage, but there were many parts that actually sustained limited damage.

Does this change how you view the image?

Lee Surrenders

Grant and Lee met and signed the **surrender** papers on April 9, 1865. Lee returned to his army and said, "Men, we have fought through the war together. I have done the best I could for you. My heart is too full to say more."

The word of Lee's surrender at Appomattox shook Jefferson Davis. With Richmond in danger, Davis and his family fled south. Davis was captured by Union troops in Georgia.

Davis Is Imprisoned

Davis was imprisoned at Fort Monroe in Virginia for two years. He was charged, but never tried, for **treason**. After his release, Davis returned to Mississippi, planning to farm the land of his **plantation**. The farm failed, and for the rest of his life, Davis relied on the support of others. He also wrote a book about the Confederacy, called *The Rise and Fall of the Confederate Government*. Davis died in 1889 at the age of 81.

WILMER MCLEAN

In an ironic twist, one man witnessed both the beginning and end of the Civil War. Wilmer McLean owned a farm in northern Virginia during the Civil War. The first Battle of Bull Run was fought across his land in 1861. A cannonball ripped through the kitchen, but no one was hurt. McLean wanted to find a place where his family would not be threatened by war. He moved to Appomattox Court House. In 1865, his home was chosen to be the site for Lee and Grant to meet for the surrender. McLean witnessed both the beginning and end of the war.

Lincoln Asks for "Dixie"

The day after Lee's surrender, April 10, 1865, Lincoln asked a band at the White House to play the southern song, "Dixie." He said, "I thought 'Dixie' one of the best tunes I ever heard..."

Grant (seated right) allowed Lee (seated left) and his soldiers to surrender with dignity and return to their homes.

The Assassination of Abraham Lincoln

Abraham Lincoln was reelected president of the United States in 1864. Just five days after Lee's surrender, Lincoln attended a play at Ford's Theatre. Driven by a hatred of the **Union** and a loyalty to the fallen Confederacy, John Wilkes Booth plotted to kill Lincoln, several members of his **cabinet**, and General Grant. He recruited others to take part in the plan. Booth burst into Lincoln's box in the middle of the play and shot him in the back of the head. Soldiers carried Lincoln from the theater to a nearby boardinghouse. Doctors could not save him, and Lincoln died early the next morning.

John Wilkes Booth was caught, but was killed while trying to escape.

As the North mourned the **assassination** of Lincoln, some in the South celebrated the death of the man they considered responsible for the war. Others realized that his absence might only mean tougher times ahead. Lincoln had already begun planning for after the war. He wanted the Southern states to be brought back into the Union without harsh punishment. Southerners did not like Lincoln, but they now possibly faced even greater difficulties under the guidance of a new president who could not control Congress.

LINCOLN'S SECOND INAUGURAL SPEECH

In his second **inaugural speech** on March 4, 1865, Lincoln spoke about how the people had tried to stop the war and preserve the Union. Now that the war was coming to an end, he begged for **leniency** for the citizens of the South.

The last paragraph of Lincoln's speech read: "With malice toward none, with charity for all, with firmness in the right as God gives us to see the right, let us strive on to finish the work we are in, to bind up the nation's wounds, to care for him who shall have borne the battle and for his widow and his orphan—to do all which may achieve and cherish a just and lasting peace among ourselves and with all nations."

Lincoln's assassination was a terrible blow to the whole nation, which now needed his leadership to heal the Union.

Can the Country Be Reunited?

After the war, slavery was officially abolished throughout the United States with the Thirteenth **Amendment** to the **Constitution**. Former slaves rejoiced at their freedom and then began to build new lives. Survival was difficult, as they had no money. Many agreed to work for their former masters, becoming **sharecroppers**. Others traveled north to try to find work. Racial tensions were still strong, so many former slaves were mistreated. The Freedman's Bureau was created to help blacks establish farms, learn to read, and start businesses.

Reconstruction

The time after the Civil War, when Southern states were brought back into the **Union**, is known as Reconstruction. President Andrew Johnson tried to carry out Lincoln's plan for restoring the Southern states to the Union. However, **Radical Republicans** controlled Congress, and they thought it should be more difficult for the rebellious Southern states to rejoin the Union. They tried to **impeach** President Johnson, then placed the South under military occupation. The 11 Southern states that had **seceded** were admitted back into the Union over the next four years. However, the military occupation of the South did not completely end until Rutherford B. Hayes took office as president of the United States in 1877, twelve years after the end of the Civil War.

Southern slaves gained their freedom at the end of the Civil War, but had little else with which to start a fresh life.

42

Carpetbaggers

Unfortunately, some men traveled from the North to make a profit from the situation in the South. They were called "**carpetbaggers**" because they often carried suitcases made of carpet material. They would buy **plantations**, farms, and businesses for the amount of taxes owed, often getting land for just pennies an acre.

New Beginnings

After the war ended, many people traveled west to start new farms and towns. Families from the North and the South often settled on farms next to each other. In time, their differences disappeared as they took pride in being American citizens.

The war had been fought to end **slavery** and to preserve the Union. Both goals had been met, and the country was again united.

The tensions that were left would take a long time to calm. Memorial Day was established to honor those who died in the Civil War, as well as in other wars. Soldiers from both sides eventually reunited in memory.

Andrew Johnson faced a difficult task when he took over for Lincoln as president of the United States.

The Southern states were admitted back to the Union over a period of four years.

STATE	DATE REJOINED THE UNION
Tennessee	July 24, 1866
Arkansas	June 22, 1868
Florida	June 25, 1868
North Carolina	July 4, 1868
Louisiana	July 9, 1868
South Carolina	July 9, 1868
Alabama	July 13, 1868
Virginia	January 26, 1870
Mississippi	February 23, 1870
Texas	March 30, 1870
Georgia	July 15, 1870

Timeline

1820	Missouri Compromise
1850	Compromise of 1850
1854	Kansas-Nebraska Act
1860	Abraham Lincoln elected president of the United States
December 1860–May 1861	Eleven Southern states secede from the Union
February 1861	Jefferson Davis is appointed president of the Confederacy
April 12, 1861	Confederate forces attack and capture Fort Sumter, beginning the Civil War
July 21, 1861	First Battle of Bull Run or Manassas
September 17, 1862	Battle of Antietam
September 1862	Lincoln signs the Emancipation Proclamation
March 9, 1862	Battle of the ironclads CSS *Virginia* and USS *Monitor*
July 4, 1863	General Grant captures Vicksburg after a long siege

February 17, 1864	The CSS *H.L Hunley* sinks the USS *Housatonic* and then also sinks

September 2, 1864	General Sherman takes Atlanta

December 21, 1864	Sherman captures Savannah

April 9, 1865	General Robert E. Lee surrenders to General Grant

April 15, 1865	President Lincoln dies after being shot by John Wilkes Booth

December 1865	Thirteenth Amendment to the Constitution ends slavery

1866–1870	Eleven Southern states are readmitted to the Union

Glossary

amendment change or addition to the United States Constitution

assassination murder of a prominent person, usually for political reasons

blockade prevent goods from entering or leaving; also used as a noun

cabinet people who advise the leader of the government and help make important decisions

carpetbaggers greedy people who took advantage of the conditions in the South to make money for themselves

civilian any person who is not in active duty in the military

compromise agreement achieved after everyone involved accepts less than they originally wanted

Confederate States of America group of 11 Southern states that seceded from the United States in 1860-1861

Constitution fundamental law of the United States that went into effect in 1789

Constitutional Convention meeting of delegates from the states in 1789 to write the Constitution and form the government the United States has today

cotton gin machine invented by Eli Whitney that picks the seeds out of cotton fibers at a much faster rate than by hand

economy system of economic activity, including commerce for producing, selling, and buying goods and services

Emancipation Proclamation document issued by President Lincoln that granted freedom to slaves living in Confederate states when those states did not return to the Union by January 1, 1863

federal related to a central or national government, as opposed to the governments of individual states

hull body or frame of a ship

immigrant person who comes to live in a new country

impeach formally remove a president of the United States, which can be done by Congress

inaugural speech talk given by the president at his swearing-in ceremony; also called the inaugural address

inflation situation where money is worth less and prices are rising

ironclad warship covered with iron plates

leniency generosity or mercy

Mexican-American War conflict between the United States and Mexico from 1846 to 1848

militia usually nonprofessional military group that take orders from a state

morale state of the soldiers' cheerfulness, discipline, and confidence

plantation large farm or estate that is worked by a large number of laborers, like slaves

Radical Republicans
Republican members of
Congress at the end of the
Civil War who tried to impeach
Andrew Johnson and make it
harder for Southern states to
rejoin the Union

ratification formal approval

Revolutionary War war
against the British for
American independence,
fought 1775–1783

secede break away from
something

sharecropper poor farmer
who uses someone else's land
and gives the owner part of
the crop in return

siege military strategy of
surrounding a city and cutting
it off from support and
supplies in order to force it
to surrender

slavery condition of a
person being owned
by another

states' rights rights and
powers the states possess
in relation to the federal
government, as guaranteed
by the Constitution

surrender quit a battle,
admitting defeat

treason crime of acting
to bring down or defeat
the government

Underground Railroad
network of secret routes used
to help slaves escape the
South to gain freedom

Union United States
of America

U.S. Senate upper body
of lawmakers of the U.S.
government, which has fewer
members who serve longer
terms than members of the
House of Representatives

Find Out More

Books

Warren, Andrea. *Under Siege*. New York: Farrar, Straus, Giroux, 2009.

Websites

http://www.nps.gov/archive/arho/tour/home.html
This is the website for Arlington House: The Robert E. Lee Memorial.

http://www.moc.org/site/PageServer
This is the website for the Museum of the Confederacy.

**http://www.co.henrico.va.us/departments/rec/recreation-centers---facilities/
meadowfarm/**
This is the website of Meadow Farm Museum.

Index